Crochet Top

10 Beautifull Designs for Your Summer

Contents

Introduction

Crochet tops are a great way for beginners to move into the space of crochet garments. They are quicker to make than crochet sweaters and are usually less complicated to crochet.

If you've never crocheted a top before, then don't worry, these cute crochet top ideas like trendy crochet tanks and crochet crop tops are the perfect gateway into learning about crochet wearables.

If you are looking for a great collection of free crochet crop tops and crochet tanks to make for Summer, then this book is for you.

Happy Crocheting!

Crochet Basics
Materials and Equipments

1. Yarn

Whether or not you consider it a crochet tool, yarn might be the most fun material on the list. Big box and chain stores will probably have the largest, most affordable selection and offer yarns you can buy all year 'round. For more specialized products and services, check out local yarn shops staffed by knowledgeable crafters.

Factors on the yarn label that can influence your project include:

Thickness (fine, medium, bulky, etc.)
Fiber content (what the yarn's made of)
Weight in ounces or grams
Length in yards or meters
Tool suggestions (hook size)
Care instructions
In choosing yarn colors, pay attention to the lot number as well as the name of the color. Because yarn is dyed in batches, subtle differences exist, even within the same color from the same brand. The lot number ensures you're getting yarn from a specific batch.

2. Hooks

Every crochet hook has a handle (where you hold on), shank (between the handle and hook head and determines the hook size) and hook head (the part that grabs the yarn). After that, the variations are endless.

The most important variation is crochet hook size, designated by letters, numbers and millimeters. The millimeters provide the universal shank diameter, and the corresponding numbers and letters reflect a measurement system unique to the United States. While you're learning, try to use hook sizes recommended on your yarn labels.

Next select the kind of hook head you need:

- Inline hook heads are in line with the hook handle and have a deep groove (throat) to give you the most control over your yarn.
- Tapered hook heads protrude beyond the hook handle and have a shallow, more rounded throat.
- Hybrid hook heads are a middle ground between inline and tapered hook heads, and considered useful for the largest range of abilities and projects.

Choosing what your hooks are made of hinges on they type of yarn you'll use:

- Metal hooks are either shiny (for grippy, acrylic yarns) or matte (for smoother animal fiber yarns).
- Plastic hooks are affordable but don't work well with acrylic yarns, as the friction between the plastics creates a lag that takes a toll on the hands.
- Wooden hooks are inexpensive, high quality and work well with a range of yarn types.

Consider the ergonomics of your hooks, including handle thickness and curve and cushioning added around the hook itself. This will likely take some trial and error to see what feels best on your hands and wrists.

3. SCISSORS

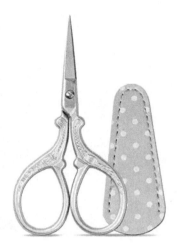

While any old scissors will work to snip your yarn, seasoned crocheters tend to prefer embroidery scissors. These small tools fit well in kits and often come in fun colors and designs.

You might also consider folding scissors as a safety and space-saving measure.

4. Tape Measure or Ruler

Keep a tape measure on hand for checking your gauge and measuring your crochet.

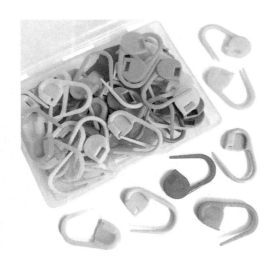

5. Stitch Markers

These can be hooked onto the crochet to mark a specific row or a specific stitch in the row, or to mark the right side of your crochet.

6. Pin cushion

A useful item to have by your side when working.

7. Row counter

These are useful for keeping track of where you are in your crochet. String on a length of cotton yarn and hang it around your neck—change it each time you complete a row.

Stitches and Techniques

Single Crochet (sc)

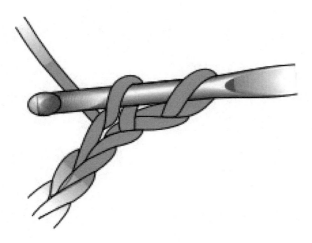

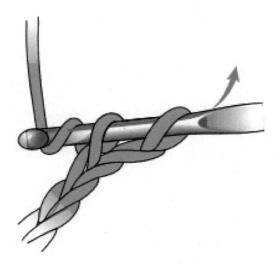

2. Yarn over again and pull the yarn through both loops on the hook.

1. Insert the hook into the work (second chain from hook on the starting chain), *yarn over and pull up a loop.

3. 1 sc made. Insert hook into next stitch; repeat from * in step 1.

Half Double Crochet (hdc)

1. *Yarn over and insert the hook into the work (third chain from hook on the starting chain).*

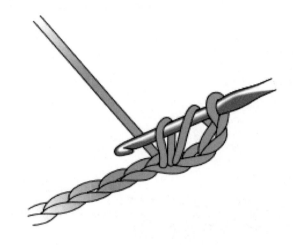

2. ** Yarn over and draw through pulling up a loop.*

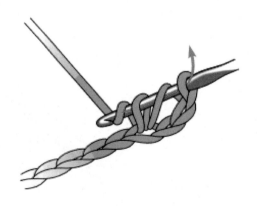

3. *Yarn over again and pull yarn through all three loops on the hook.*

4. *1 hdc made. Yarn over, insert hook into next stitch; repeat from * in step 2.*

Double Crochet (dc)

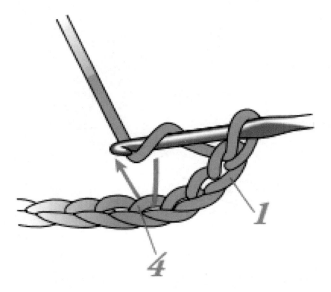

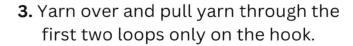

1. Yarn over and insert the hook into the work (fourth hain from hook on starting chain).

2. * Yarn over and draw yarn through pulling up a loop.

3. Yarn over and pull yarn through the first two loops only on the hook.

9

4. Yarn over and pull yarn through the last two loops on the hook.

5. 1 dc made. Yarn over, insert hook into next stitch; repeat from * in Step 2.

Treble (tr)

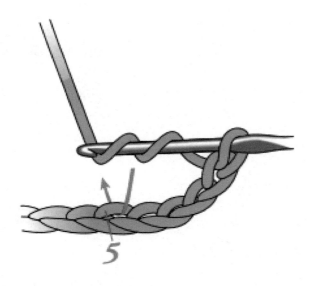

1. Yarn over twice, insert the hook into the work (fifth chain from hook on the starting chain).

2. * Yarn over and draw yarn through pulling up a loop.

3. Yarn over again and pull yarn through the first two loops only on the hook.

11

4. Yarn over again and pull yarn through
the next two loops only on the hook.

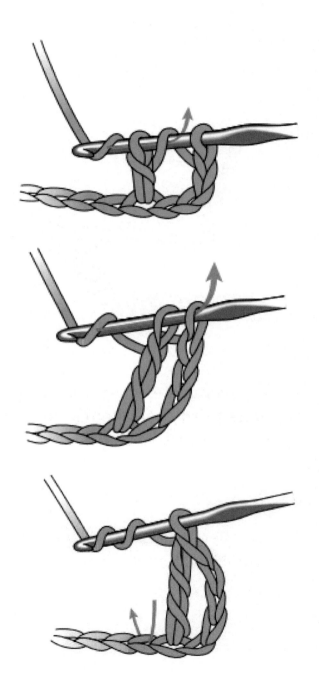

5. Yarn over again and pull yarn through
the last two loops on the hook.

6. 1 tr made. Yarn over twice, insert hook into next stitch; repeat from * in Step 2.

Special Stitches

Foundation Half Double Crochet:

*Note – If using the FHDC for the first time.

Ch 2, yarn over, insert your hook into the first chain.
Yarn over and pull up one loop (You should have three loops on your hook).
Yarn over and pull through the first loop on your hook (This creates the 'chain' of the FHDC).
Yarn over and pull through all three loops (You should have one loop on your hook).
You have created your first single crochet.

*Yarn over, insert your hook in between the chain and HDC.
Yarn over and pull up one loop (Three loops on your hook)
Yarn over and pull through the first loop on your hook.
Yarn over and pull through all three loops. ;
Repeat from * until you have the desired number of stitches.

Abbreviations

ch = chain

sc = single crochet

sc2tog = single crochet two together

sc3tog = single crochet three together

BLO = back loop only

rep =. repeat

Sl st = Slip Stitch

FHDC = Foundation Half Double Crochet

HDC = Half Double Crochet

DC = Double Crochet

Inc = increase

Dec = decrease

RS = right side

ch-sp = Chain-space

sk = skip

2sc tog = 2 single crochet together (decrease)

2dc tog = 2 double crochet together (decrease)

dc2tog = double crochet 2 stitches together

FDC = foundation double crochet

PM = place marker

4dcshell = place 4 dc all into same st

FO= fasten off

Cont = continue

FpDC = Front Post Double Crochet

BpDC = Back Post Double Crochet

Crochet Top Patterns

Hepaticagranny Top

MATERIALS:

- 4,5 mm / US size 7 hook
- darning needle, scissors
- About 300 m worsted weight cotton yarn. I used Julie från Falkgarn: 3 skeins in 10 ecru, one skein each of 14 blue, and 15 green.

Gauge

One granny square = 10x10 cm / 4x4 inches
14 sc x 18 rows = 10x10 cm / 4x4 inches

Sizes

- S/M: chest measurement up to 90 cm / 35 inches
-
- M/L: chest measurement c. 95-105 cm / 37-41 inches
- The final size of the top depends on the number of granny squares you start with.
- above is about a size S/M and starts with a strip of 7 granny squares (each square being c. 10x10 cm / 4x4 inches).
- The top is quite elastic and is adjusted / done up with ties at the back, so one size can fit many shapes.
- The solid sc top part is c. 20 cm / 8 inches high in top (S/M), i.e. from neck down to under the bust.
- If you begin with a strip of 8 squares (M/L), the solid top part will be c. 25 cm / 10 inches. You can of course experiment using fewer or more granny squares to get smaller or larger sizes.

PATTERN

1. The Granny Squares

Round 1: (white) start with a magic ring, or ch4 & join with a slst to form a ring. Ch2, dc into the ring (counts as the first 2dc tog), ch1, [2dc tog, ch1] 7 times into the ring. Close with a slst in the first st. Now you should have 8 'petals' (=2dc tog), each separated by 1 ch.
Fasten off.

Round 2: (blue/green) insert hook into the chsp in-between two 'petals' & pull up a loop, ch3 (counts as first dc), 2 dc in the same ch-sp, ch1, [3 dc in next ch-sp, ch1] 7 times, close with a slst in the first dc. Now you should have 8 dc groups, each separated by 1 ch. Fasten off.

Round 3: (white) insert hook into the ch-sp inbetween two 'petals' (dc-groups) & pull up a loop, ch 5 (counts as first dc + 2 ch), 3 dc in the same ch-sp, ch1, *3 dc in next ch-sp, ch1, [3 dc, ch2, 3 dc, ch1] in next ch-sp, repeat from * 2 more times, 3 dc in next ch-sp, ch1, 2 dc in next ch-sp (where you started), close with a slst in the first dc.
Now your circle will have become a square with 2 dc groups in each corner, and one dc group on each side of the square.

Round 4: (white) slst to the next corner ch-sp, ch 3 (counts as the first dc), [dc, ch2, 3 dc, ch1] in the same ch-sp, *3 dc in next ch-sp, ch1, 3 dc in next ch-sp, ch1, [3 dc, ch2, 3 dc, ch1] in next corner ch-sp, repeat from * 2 more times, 3 dc in next ch-sp, ch1, 3 dc in next ch-sp, ch1, dc in next ch-sp (where you started), close with a slst in the first dc. Fasten off.

Make 7 squares for size S/M, 8 squares for M/L.
Sew or crochet together the squares to form a long strip. There are countless ways to join granny squares.

2. The Top Part

Row 1: now we're going to work a row of sc along the long edge of your granny strip. Put the strip horizontally in front of you,right side up, insert hook in the top right corner ch-sp (top left if you're left handed), pull up a loop, ch1 (does not count as a st), 2 sc in the same ch-sp, now sc into each dc along the edge, plus 1 sc into each of the joins in-between the squares. (Sk the ch-sp's in-between the dc-groups.) In the final corner ch-sp in the top left corner of the granny strip, work 1 sc if your strip has 7 squares; work 2 sc if your strip has 8 squares. Turn. (Total of 93 sc for 7-squarestrip; 107 sc for 8-square-strip: exact st count not that important as long as you end up with an uneven no. of sts.)

Row 2: ch4 (counts as dc + ch1), sk next st, [dc in next st, ch1, skip next st] repeat to end of row, finish with a dc in the last st, turn.

Row 3: ch1 (does not count as a st), sc in each st (dcs as well as ch-sp's) across, turn.

Row 4: now we'll start decreasing: ch1 (does not count as a st), sk first st, sc in next st & in each st

across up to the final 2 sts, 2sc tog into the final 2 sts, turn.

Repeat row 4 c. 35 times, or until the row has shrunk to about 12-15 cm / 5-6 inches. Make sure to

have an uneven no. of sts before continuing to the finishing rows.

Finishing row 1: ch4 (counts as dc + ch1), sk next st, [dc in next st, ch1, skip next st] repeat to end of row, finish with a dc in the last st, turn.

Finishing row 2: ch1 (does not count as a st), sc in each st (dcs as well as ch-sp's) across. Fasten off

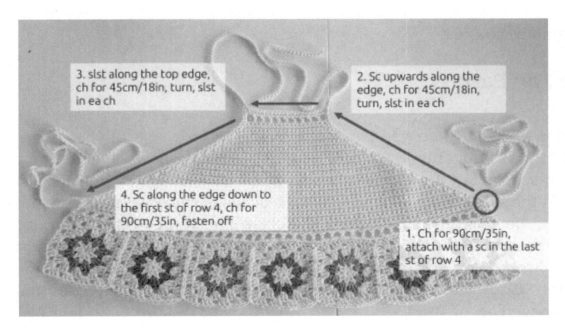

3. slst along the top edge, ch for 45cm/18in, turn, slst in ea ch

2. Sc upwards along the edge, ch for 45cm/18in, turn, slst in ea ch

4. Sc along the edge down to the first st of row 4, ch for 90cm/35in, fasten off

1. Ch for 90cm/35in, attach with a sc in the last st of row 4

3. Edging Row & Ties

Work a 90 cm / 35 inches long chain, sc into the last st of row 4 (circled in photo below), sc into the side of each row of the top part, working in the direction of the red arrow (see photo) up to the top corner, work a 45 cm / 18 inches long chain, turn, slst into each ch all the way back to the corner, slst into each st along the top edge, work another 45 cm / 18 inches long chain, turn, slst into each ch back to the corner, sc into the side of each row of the top part, working your way down along the edge, finishing in the first st from row 4, work a second 90 cm / 35 inches long chain. Fasten off and weave in the ends.

Thread the long chain ties through the sts at the back as in the photo:

Chasing Summer Tank Top

MATERIALS:

- Yarn: DK—WeCrochet CotLin in Cashew
- 70% Tanguis Cotton, 30% Linen
- 123 yds [112 m] per 1.76-oz [50 g] skein
- Only $4.99 per skein

- **Yardage**: 2 (3, 3, 3, 4) (4, 5, 5, 6) skeins of CotLin or 225 (275, 300, 350, 400) (450, 500, 600, 675) yds [206 (252, 275, 321, 366) (412, 458, 549, 618) m] of a similar, DK weight yarn.

- **Hook**: Size U.S. E/4 (3.5 mm) or size needed to obtain gauge

Gauge

4 x 4″ [10 x 10 cm] = 19 sts and 9 rows in Double Crochet

Sizing

This pattern is written in 9 sizes: XS (S, M, L, XL) (2X, 3X, 4X, 5X) to fit bust sizes 28-30 (32-34, 36-38, 40-42, 44-46) (48-50, 52-54, 56-58, 60-62)“. If you're unsure which size you fall under, you can check out this sizing chart. For this pattern, if you're in between sizes, size down.

PATTERN

FRONT PANEL (Make 2)

Leaving a long tail for seaming, FDC 34 (36, 36, 38, 40) (42, 44, 48, 50). For a longer (or shorter) tank top than sample shown, work a longer (or shorter) chain here.

Row 1 (Set-Up Row): Ch 2, dc in each st to end of row, work 5 dc in end of last st (see Fig. 1 below), PM in 3rd dc of this 5-dc cluster, continue working in the same direction down your foundation chain, work 34 (36, 36, 38, 40) (42, 44, 48, 50) dc to end of row, turn. [73 (77, 77, 81, 85) (89, 93, 101, 105) dc]

work 5 dc in this space

Row 2: Ch 2, dc in each st to marked st, work 5 dc in marked st, PM in 3rd dc of this 5-dc cluster, continue dc in each st to end of row. [77 (81, 81, 85, 89) (93, 97, 105, 109) dc]

Rep last row 5 (6, 7, 8, 8) (9, 10, 11, 12) more times, or until your piece measures approximately 6.5 (7.5, 8.5, 9.5, 9.5) (10.25, 11, 12, 13)" [16.5 (19, 21.5, 24, 24) (26, 28, 30.5, 33) cm] in width.

Each Row 2 rep increases your stitch count by 4.

You should finish with 97 (105, 109, 117, 121) (129, 137, 149, 157) dc in your final row, unless you adjusted the number of Row 2 reps.

Fasten off, leaving long tail for seaming.

Rep all instructions for an identical panel, but do not fasten off after completing your second panel. Place a stitch marker in this active loop and proceed to Seaming Your Front Panels Together. You will come back to this loop to work the Back Panel.

Seaming Your Front Panels Together

Lay both of your panels flat with the same side facing you and the long tail you left after finishing the first panel in the center. You will use this tail to seam your pieces together.

With a tapestry needle and your long tail, seam your panels together using the whip stitch or seaming method of your choice. Stop at approximately 1 (1.5, 1.5, 1.5, 2) (2, 2.5, 2.5, 3)" [2.5 (4, 4, 4, 5) (5, 6, 6, 8) cm] past the length of your initial foundation chain. The height at which you stop seaming is what determines your neckline depth. Do not weave in this end yet, you will come back to it once your top is seamed together in case you need to make any adjustments to this neckline.

BACK PANEL

Return to the live loop from your second front panel and insert your hook to continue crocheting.

Row 1: Ch 2, dc in next 33 (35, 35, 37, 39) (41, 43, 47, 49) sts, dc2tog, turn. [34 (36, 36, 38, 40) (42, 44, 48, 50) dc]
Note: If you adjusted your front panel foundation chain, adjust this number of back panel stitches by the same amount. For example, if you worked 10 additional foundation double crochets, add 10 double crochets to this Row 1 stitch count.

Row 2: Ch 2, sk first dc, dc in each st to end of row, turn. [33 (35, 35, 37, 39) (41, 43, 47, 49) dc]

Row 3: Ch 2, dc in each st to end of row, turn.
Rep Row 3 until you have worked a total of 32 (37, 42, 47, 56) (61, 66, 71, 76) rows across your back panel.
Next Row (S, L, 2X, 4X): Ch 2, dc in each st to last st, work 2 dc in last st.

Next Row (XS, M, XL, 3X, 5X): Ch 2, work 2 dc in first st, dc in each st to end of row.

Your back panel width should measure approximately 14.5 (17, 19, 21.5, 25.5) (27.5, 30, 32, 34)" [37 (43, 48, 55, 65) (70, 76, 81, 86) cm].

Fasten off, leaving long tail for seaming panels together.

Seaming Your Tank Top

Optional: To double-check your fit before seaming, you can pin your top into a tube with locking stitch markers and try it on. Bring the last back panel row together with your front panel. Pin these stitches together lengthwise. Try on your top before seaming it closed and adjust the number of rows on your back panel if needed. For a tighter top, rip out a few rows; if your top is too tight, work additional Row 2 reps until reaching your desired circumference.

With a tapestry needle use your long tail to seam your panels together into a tube using the whip stitch or seaming method of your choice. Weave in ends.

Bottom Finishing Row

Next, you will work a row of single crochet along the bottom edge for a neater finish.

Join yarn somewhere on the side of your tank top to the bottom edge with a sl st, ch 1, work 2 sc for every dc row-end until reaching your starting point, sl st into first sc to join, fasten off, weave in ends.

STRAPS

Choose which side you'd like to wear as the front and lay your top so that this Right Side is facing down, and the back of your top is toward you.

Place a stitch marker into the top edge of your Back Panel to mark the true center-back. Being mindful of this center point, place two additional markers on either side of the center marker at equal distances apart to mark out where you would like your straps to be.

You can remove your center marker now.
Join new yarn to the right-most marker with a sl st.

Ch 1, sc across to opposite marker by working approximately 2 sc into each dc row-end.

28

For longer (or shorter) straps, work a longer (or shorter) chain than instructed below.

Ch 50, sc into the center marked st on your front panel to join your strap to the front, sc in each dc, working toward the center-front of your top, continue to sc into each dc until reaching the center marked st on your other front panel, sc into this marked st, ch 50, sc into the marked st that you started with. You should be at your starting point. Sl st into your first sc to join.

Before fastening off, try on your top to make sure you are happy with the strap length. Adjust if necessary. Once satisfied with strap length, fasten off. At this point, you can also adjust your center-front seam to your desired height, now that you can see how the tank top lays on your body. Weave in ends.

Strap Finishing Rows

Next, you will work a row of sc along the straps and the raw edges at the underarm for a neater finish.
Lay your tank top in the same orientation as you did when working the straps, with your Right Side facing down, and the back of your top toward you (as shown in the photos below).

First Side

Join new yarn to the left of the strap on your left with a sl st. Sc into each st along the back working 2 sc for every dc row-end, continue to sc into each dc from your front panel until reaching the strap. Sc into the back-bumps of each ch until reaching your starting point, sl st into first sc to join, fasten off, weave in ends.

Second Side

Join new yarn to the right of the strap on your right with a sl st. Sc into the back-bumps of each ch, sc into each dc along the front panel until reaching the dc row-ends from the back panel, work 2 sc for every dc row-end until reaching your starting point, sl st into first sc to join, fasten off, weave in ends.

Weave in any remaining ends, block to dimensions in chart.

Summer Flower Top

Materials and Specifications

- **Tools**: Crochet hook 3.0 mm* or 3.5 mm.
- **Yarns:**

Scheepjes Stone Washed – River Washed yarn pack*

Novita Cotton Soft in color "noki" (099) 2 balls (XS/S), 2-3 balls (S/M) or other black DK/sport-weight yarns such as Lion Brand 24/7 Cotton* or Drops Safran*.

Instead of Scheepjes yarn pack you can also purchase Scheepjes Stone Washed yarn balls* or Scheepjes River Washed yarn balls* separately.

The finished top in size XS-S measures approx. 71 cm when not stretched and in size S-M it measures approx. 80 cm when not stretched. The side length of a smaller square measures 11,5 cm and the diagonal measures 15 cm.

PATTERN

Flower Granny Square

Start the flower granny square doing a magic loop with the first color (XYZN). XYZN represents the color order of the square so that X represents the yarn color of the first round, Y represents the second round's color and so on. N represents black yarn that finishes the square. The bolded letter in XYZN indicates the yarn color that is used in the following round.

Round 1: Chain 4 into the loop (this counts as the 1st treble (tr) crochet stitch). Insert a treble crochet and pull the yarn through both loops on your hook. Close the cluster with a chain stitch and chain one (1). *Crochet a 2-tr-cluster: insert a tr into the loop but do not pull the yarn through the last two loops on your hook. Instead, insert the second tr and pull the yarn through until you have three (3) loops on your hook. Pull the yarn through all of them and close the cluster with a chain. Chain 1.* Repeat * 10 more times. Pull the tail end of the yarn and close the round with a slip stitch (sl st) to the top of the first cluster. You now have 12 clusters in a magic loop.

Change the color (XYZN).

Round 2. Crochet a slip stitch to the chain between the first and the second tr-cluster. Chain 3 (this counts as the 1st double (dc) crochet stitch). Insert a dc and pull the yarn through both loops on your hook. Close the cluster with a chain stitch and chain one (1). *Crochet a 2-dc-cluster: insert a dc to the chain between the second and the third tr-cluster but do not pull the yarn through both loops on your hook. Instead, insert the second dc and pull the yarn through until you have three (3) loops on your hook. Pull the yarn through all of them and close the cluster with a chain. Chain 1. Now, insert two 2-dc-clusters to the chain between the third and the fourth tr-cluster (close the first 2-dc-cluster with a chain and chain 1. Insert the second 2-dc-cluster and close it with a chain and chain 1.)* Repeat * 3 more times. Close the round with a sl st to the top of the first cluster.

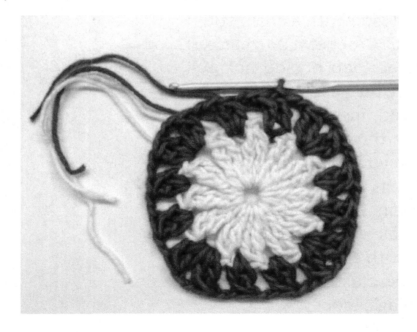

34

Change the color (XYZN).

Round 3. Crochet a slip stitch to the chain between the first and the second dc-cluster. Chain 3 (this counts as the first dc). Insert a dc but do not pull the yarn through the last two loops. Instead, insert the third dc and pull the yarn through until you have three (3) loops on your hook. Pull the yarn through all of them and close the cluster with a chain. Chain 1. *Crochet a 3-dc-cluster: insert a dc to the chain between the second and the third dc-cluster but do not pull the yarn through both loops on your hook.
 Instead, insert the second dc and pull the yarn through until you have three (3) loops on your hook. Insert the third dc and pull the yarn through until you have four (4) loops on your hook. Pull the yarn through all of them and close the cluster with a chain. Chain 1. Now, insert two 3-dc-clusters to the chain between the two 2-dc clusters (close the first 3-dc-cluster with a chain and chain 1. Insert the second 3-dc-cluster and close it with a chain and chain 1.)
Insert one 3-dc-cluster to the next chain between 2-dc-clusters as described earlier. Insert another 3-dc-cluster to the next chain.* Repeat * 3 more times (except in the last repetition time, do not follow the last sentence of *). Close the round with a sl st to the top of the first cluster.

35

Change the color to black (XYZN).

Round 4. Crochet a slip stitch to the chain between the first and the second 3-dc-cluster. Insert the first 3-dc-shell: chain 3 (this counts as the first dc) and insert two dcs to that same chain between the first and the second 3-dc-cluster. Move on forward to the chain between the second and the third 3-dc-cluster and insert a 3-dc-shell (no chaining between the shells). *Now after a total of two 3-dc-shells, insert two 3-tr-shells to the chain between the two 3-dc-clusters and chain 1 between these 3-tr-shells. Insert a total of four (4) 3-dc-shells to each chain between 3-dc-clusters of the round 3.* Repeat * 3 more times. Insert two 3-tr-shells the the last corner as described earlier and then insert 3-dc-shells to each chain before the end of the round. Close the round with a sl st to the top of the chained dc.

36

For size XS/S the flower granny square is now finished. For larger size (S/M) follow the round 5: Use the same color again (XYZNN).

FOR SIZE S/M: Round 5. Repeat the round 4 so that you insert 3-dc-shells to every space between previous round's 3-dc-shells and two 3-tr-shells to the chain between previous round's 3-tr-shells.
Figure 9. The round 5 of the granny square (for size S/M).
Crochet a total of 12 flower granny squares according to the table in the Figure 2.

Flower Granny Triangle
Crochet triangle pattern
Figure 10. The triangle crochet pattern.

Crochet three (3) flower granny triangles. You can find the color order for the triangles in the Figure 2. Start the triangle doing a magic loop with the first color (XYZN).

Triangle round 1: Chain 4 into the loop (this counts as the 1st treble (tr) crochet stitch). Insert a treble crochet and pull the yarn through both loops on your hook. Close the cluster with a chain stitch and chain one (1). *Crochet a 2-tr-cluster: insert a tr into the loop but do not pull the yarn through the last two loops on your hook. Instead, insert the second tr and pull the yarn through until you have three (3) loops on your hook. Pull the yarn through all of them and close the cluster with a chain. Chain 1.* Repeat * 4 more times. Pull the tail end of the yarn so that the clusters form a half circle. You now have 6 clusters in a magic loop.

Figure 11. The round 1 of the triangle.

Change the color (XYZN).

Triangle round 2. Chain 3 (this counts as the 1st double (dc) crochet stitch) and turn the work around. Insert a dc to the top of previous round's 2-tr-cluster right next to the 3 chains and pull the yarn through both loops on your hook. Close the cluster with a chain stitch and chain one (1). *Crochet a 2-dc-cluster: insert a dc to the chain between the first and the second 2-tr-cluster but do not pull the yarn through both loops on your hook. Instead, insert the second dc and pull the yarn through until you have three (3) loops on your hook. Pull the yarn through all of them and close the cluster with a chain. Chain 1.* Repeat * one more time. Now, insert two 2-dc-clusters to the chain between the third and the fourth 2-tr-cluster (close the first 2-dc-cluster with a chain and chain 1. After the second 2-dc-cluster, close it with a chain and chain 1). Then repeat * 3 more times but do the last 2-dc-cluster to the top of previous round's 2-tr-cluster.

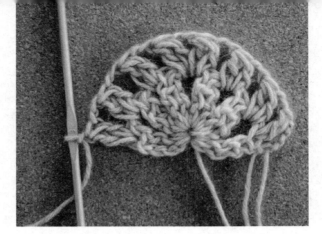

Figure 12. The round 2 of the triangle.

Change the color (XYZN).

Triangle round 3. Chain 3 (this counts as the 1st double (dc) crochet stitch) and turn the work around. Insert a dc to the top of previous round's 2-dc-cluster right next to the 3 chains but do not pull the yarn through the last two loops. Instead, insert the third dc to the same loop as the second dc and pull the yarn through until you have three (3) loops on your hook. Pull the yarn through all of them and close the cluster with a chain. Chain 1. *Crochet a 3-dc-cluster: insert a dc to the chain between the first and the second 2-dc-cluster but do not pull the yarn through both loops on your hook. Instead, insert the second dc and pull the yarn through until you have three (3) loops on your hook. Insert the third dc and pull the yarn through until you have four (4) loops on your hook. Pull the yarn through all of them and close the cluster with a chain. Chain 1.* Repeat * two more times. Now, insert two 3-dc-clusters to the chain between the two 2-dc clusters (close the first 3-dc-cluster with a chain and chain 1. Insert the second 3-dc-cluster and close it with a chain and chain 1.) Then repeat * 4 more times but do the last 3-dc-cluster to the top of previous round's 2-dc-cluster.

Figure 13. The round 3 of the triangle.

Change the color to black (XYZN).

Triangle round 4. Chain 4 and this time, do not turn the work around. From now on, you will work around the triangle. The 4 chains belong to the last cluster of this round. Base side: Now, you will work the base side (the longest side) of the triangle. Insert three (3) dc stitches to the last dc of the triangle round 3. These three dcs form a 3-dc-shell. Move on forward to the next space (the 3 chains of the triangle round 2) and insert a 3-dc-shell (no chaining between). Move on to the last tr of the triangle round 1 and insert a 3-dc-shell. Now after a total of three 3-dc-shells, chain 1 and insert another three 3-dc-shells to the corresponding spaces as the first three 3-dc-shells. Next comes the right corner: insert two 3-tr-shells to the top of the first 3-dc-cluster of the previous round (round 3) and chain 1 between the 3-tr-shells. Next comes the right side: insert a total of four (4) 3-dc-shells to each chain between 3-dc-clusters of triangle round 3. Next comes the top corner: insert two 3-tr-shells (chain 1 between the 3-tr-shells) to the chain between two 3-dc-clusters of the triangle round 3.

Next comes the left side: insert a total of four (4) 3-dc-shells to each chain between 3-dc-clusters of triangle round 3. Next comes the left corner: insert two 3-tr-shells to the top of the last 3-dc-cluster of the previous round (round 3) and chain 1 between the 3-tr-shells, **NOTE**: in the second 3-tr-cluster, do not insert the third tr because you have already chained one tr in the beginning of this round. Close the round with a sl st to the top of this chained tr.

Figure 14. The round 4 of the triangle.

For size XS/S the flower granny triangle is now finished. For larger size (S/M) follow the round 5: Use the same color again (XYZNN).

FOR SIZE S/M: Triangle round 5. Repeat the round 4 so that you insert 3-dc-shells to every space between previous round's 3-dc-shells and that you insert two 3-tr-shells to the chain between previous round's 3-tr-shells.

Figure 15. The round 5 of the triangle.

Joining Granny Squares and Triangles

Next step is to join squares and triangles together. I used the flat slip stitch joining method and I used the black yarn for joining.

The Figure 16 below shows how to assemble the squares and triangles. Note that there are only three triangles, the back hem of the top will be left "open" as you can see in the Figure 16.

Figure 16. Assembly of the squares and triangles from front and back of the top.

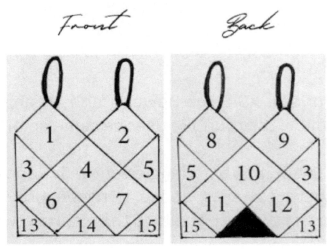

Join the granny squares and triangles so that you crochet two sides together from bottom to top and then the next two parallel sides together and so on. Then join those sides together that are perpendicularly to the first sides.

Start joining the granny squares and triangles together first from the chains of 3-tr-shells and then move on to the loops. Crochet flat slip stitches until you reach the 3-tr-shell chains again and crochet one flat slip stitch to those chains too. Then move on straight to the next squares without chaining between. When you have joined all squares parallelry, start joining the other sides. When you reach the perpendicular flat slip stitch seam, chain 1 and cross over it. Start joining the next squares together first from the chains of 3-tr-shells and then move on to the loops.

Straps and Finalizing Edges

After you have joined all the granny squares and triangles together the next step is to crochet the shoulder straps. Start from the top corner of the square from the back side of the top and chain 40 (you can also test what length is best for you). Join the strap with a slip stitch to the corresponding top corner of the square from the front side and cut the yarn. Do the same thing to the other shoulder strap but this time do not cut the yarn. Now, you finalize the edges and the straps by crocheting slip stitches first along the front neckline, then along the first strap you chained, then along the back neckline and finally along the second strap. Cut the yarn and close the round with additional slip stitch. Finalize them hem edge with slip stitches. Weave in the ends.

Tie Strap Crop Top

MATERIALS

- Yarn – Lana Grossa 365 Cotone – Aran/Worsted (10 ply), 140m/50g, 88% Cotton, 12% Polyamide, Rose (048)
- XS = 2 skeins, S = 3 skeins, M = 4 skeins, L = 4 skeins, XL = 5 skeins, 2XL = 6 skeins, 3XL = 7 skeins
- 4mm (US G) Crochet Hook
- Darning Needle
- Scissors

GAUGE: 10cm/4" square = 16 stitches wide x 16 rows tall in half double crochet

MEASUREMENTS cm:

Upper Bust: 64, 74, 84, 94, 104, 114, 124
To fit Bust: 76, 86, 96, 106, 116, 126, 136
Length: 23, 25.5, 28, 30.5, 33, 35.5, 38
Strap length: 40, 42.5, 45, 47.5, 50, 52.5, 55

MEASUREMENTS inches:

Upper Bust: 25, 29, 33, 37, 41, 45, 49
To fit Bust: 30, 34, 38, 42, 45.5, 49.5, 53.5
Length: 9, 10, 11, 12, 13, 14, 15
Strap length: 15.5, 16.5, 17.5, 18.5, 19.5, 20.5, 21.5

PATTERN

BODY

FOUNDATION CHAIN + ROUND 1: FHDC 100(116, 132, 148, 164, 180, 196), sl st into the 1st FHDC.
<100, 116, 132, 148, 164, 180, 196 >
*Wrap the Foundation Half Double Crochet Chain around your bust to double check that the top will fit (It's ok to stretch the chain).

ROUND 2: Ch 1, turn, HDC 100(116, 132, 148, 164, 180, 196), sl st into 1st HDC.
Repeat ROUND 2 until ROUND 37(41, 45, 49, 53, 57, 61).
*You can add or remove rounds to reach your desired length.

FINAL ROUND: Turn, *Ch 7 (counts as a stitch), skip 3 stitches, sl st into the next stitch; rep from * until end, sl st into the first st of the round. Fasten off. You should finish with < 25, 29, 33, 37, 41, 45, 49 > scallops.

STRAPS

FOUNDATION CHAIN: Ch 7
ROW 1: DC into the 3rd chain from the hook, DC 4. <5>
ROW 2: Ch 2, turn, DC 5. <5>
Repeat ROW 2 until ROW 40(42, 44, 46, 48, 50, 52). Fasten off.

Repeat STRAPS instructions until you have 4 straps.

*Alternatively, you can create 2 straps and have 2 plain straps instead of the tie straps. Suggest safety pinning the straps to the top and trying on the garment. Since plain straps are not adjustable, you may need to add or remove rows to reach your desired strap length.

ASSEMBLY

Fold the top in half with the front facing you. Measure in 4cm from the sides of top and pin the straps into place.

Turn the top over, (the back and seam should be facing you). Measure 5cm from the sides of the top and pin the straps into place.

Sew the straps to the top.

Weave in all of your ends.

***Note** – Along the body seam, sew the corners of the first and last Foundation Half Double Crochets together.

Little Girl Summer Top

MATERIALS

- Schachenmayr Catania Originals
- Yarn weight 2 (fine)
- The needle

Gauge

23 dc = 10 cm (4″)

10 rows = 10 cm (4″)

PATTERN

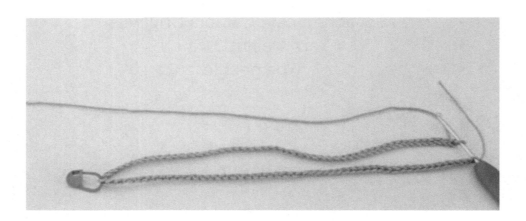

Row 1

Ch 2, 1 dc in the same stitch, 1 dc in each st to the center (the marked stitch). In the marked st 1 inc* 1 dc in each st until the last one. In the last st make 2 dc, ch 3, 1 dc and then sl st with the first dc.

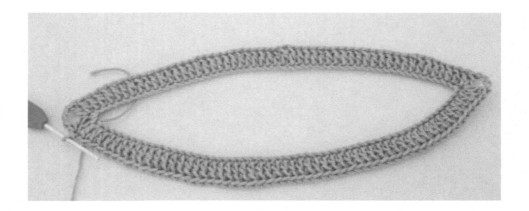

Row 2

Ch 4, [skip the next st, 1 dc, ch 1] – repeat to the center. In the 3 ch space from the center make one inc* but for the filet row

Continue with ch 1, 1 dc in the next st, ch 1, skip 1 st, 1 dc in the next. Repeat until the ch 3 space at the end of the row. Here in the chain 3 space, make 1 dc, ch 3, 1 dc, ch 1 and sl st with the 3rd st of the starting chain.

Row 3
Repeat row 2

Row 4
Repeat row 1
After first 4 rows we will work the back and front separately to form the arm hole.

Counting from the center point:
2 years – count 22 sts on the left and 22 on the right, also on the back and front side. Mark the st number 22.
4 years – 24 sts
6 years 26 sts

Row 6 front side

Skip the next st, 1 dc in the next, ch 1, skip 1, 1 dc in the next. Repeat to the center point. 1 inc in the center. Then continue with the stitch pattern to the end of the row.

Row 7 front side

Repeat row 6

Row 8 front side

Repeat row 5

Repeat the 4 rows until you have:

2 years – 12 rows in total
4 years – 14 rows
6 years – 16 rows
Repeat the same with the back side.

Row 13/15/17

At this row we will join the back and front on the side edges and we will continue to work in rounds.

Begin your work in one side and make sure you are on the right side. Work the row as normal until you get to the other side edge. Here join with the back. Continue the row to the end and here join with the front side.

Row 14/16/18

Slip st 2 sts, then start the row as normal. When you get to the side edge make a decrease (skip 3 sts from the middle) continue with the stitch pattern to the end of the row. At the end of the row decrease again, skip 3 sts then sl st.

Continue working like this until you get to the desired length.

We decrease on the side edges to have them straight considering the increase that we make in the center point of the back and front side.

Milla Crochet Tank Top

MATERIALS

3 (3, 3, 4, 4, 4, 5, 5) skeins Lion Brand Yarn Cobblestone in Fallen Rock
Size US H/8 (5mm) crochet hook
Size US I/9 (5.5mm) crochet hook
Removable stitch markers
Tapestry needle

FINISHED SIZE:

Bust/body circumference: 30"/76cm (34.5"/88cm, 39"/99cm, 43.5"/110.5cm,
48"/122cm, 52.5"/133.5cm, 57"/145cm, 61.5"/156cm)
Length: 20.5"/52cm (21"/53.5cm, 22"/56cm, 22.5"/57cm, 23.5"/57cm,
24"/26.5cm, 25"/63.5cm, 26"/66cm)
Body length: 14"/35.5cm (14"/35.5cm, 14.5"/37cm, 14.5"/37cm, 15"/38cm,
15"/38cm, 15.5"/39.5cm, 16"/40.5cm)
Armhole depth: 6.5"/16.5cm (7"/18cm, 7.5"/19cm, 8"/20.5cm, 8.5"/21.5cm,
9"/23cm, 9.5"/24cm, 10"/25.5cm)

Suggested ease: (-)2 - (+)2" / (-)5 - (+)5cm
Pictured in size S on model with 34"/86cm bust

GAUGE:

13 sts + 11 rows = 4"/10cm in half double crochet with US I/9 (5.5mm) crochet
hook

PATTERN

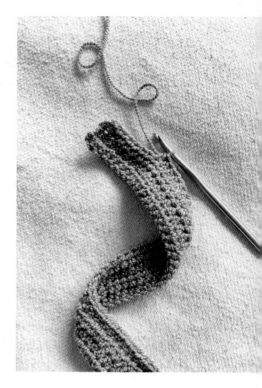

Notes: Tank is worked flat in back and forth rows and seamed. Turn at the end of each row. The ch 2 at the beginning of each row does not count as a stitch.

Back:

Bottom edging:

With smaller hook and leaving a long tail for seaming, ch 12.

Row 1 (RS): Starting in 3rd ch from hook, hdc across. (10 sts)

Row 2: Sl st loosely across.

Row 3: Ch 2, hdc across.

Rep rows 2 and 3 until work measures 15"/38cm (17.25"/44cm, 19.5"/49.5cm, 21.75"/55cm, 24"/61cm, 26.25"/66.5cm, 28.5"/72.5cm, 30.75"/78cm), ending with a row 3. Do not fasten off.

Body:

Change to larger hook. With RS facing and working along side edge of ribbing, ch 2 and hdc 50 (56, 64, 70, 78, 86, 92, 100) evenly across to other end.

Row 1: Ch 2, hdc across.

Rep row 1 until work measures 14"/35.5cm (14"/35.5cm, 14.5"/37cm, 14.5"/37cm, 15"/38cm, 15"/38cm, 15.5"/39.5cm, 16"/40.5cm) ending with a RS row. Fasten off.

Front:

Work as for back but do not fasten off.

Next 2 rows: Sl st 2 (2, 4, 4, 6, 6, 8, 12), sc 4 (4, 5, 5, 5, 5, 5, 5), hdc 4 (5, 5, 5, 6, 6, 6, 6), dc 5 (6, 6, 7, 7, 9, 10, 10), hdc 4 (5, 5, 5, 6, 6, 6, 6), sc 4 (4, 5, 5, 5, 5, 5, 5), sl st 4 (4, 4, 8, 8, 12, 12, 12), sc 4 (4, 5, 5, 5, 5, 5, 5), hdc 4 (5, 5, 5, 6, 6, 6, 6), dc 5 (6, 6, 7, 7, 9, 10, 10), hdc 4 (5, 5, 5, 6, 6, 6, 6), sc 4 (4, 5, 5, 5, 5, 5, 5), sl st 2 (2, 4, 4, 6, 6, 8, 12).
Fasten off.

Construction:

Using long tails from beginning, seam sides from top of ribbing to underarms, leaving a split vent at the bottom sides.
Left strap:

With RS facing and with smaller hook, rejoin yarn in 1st (1st, 1st, 2nd, 2nd, 2nd, 2nd, 2nd) dc at top of left bust and ch 2.
Row 1: Starting in same st as ch 2, hdc 5 (6, 6, 5, 5, 7, 8, 8) across.
Row 2: Sl st loosely across.
Row 3: Ch 2, hdc across.

Rep rows 2 and 3 until strap measures 13"/33cm (14"/35.5cm, 15"/38cm, 16"/40.5cm, 17"/43cm, 18"/45.5cm, 19"/48cm, 20"/51cm), ending with a row 3. Do not fasten off.

Lay tank flat with the back facing up and fold the strap over, lining it up to the back top edge. Sl st through the top edge of the back and the last row of the strap together to attach.

Right strap:

Work as for left strap along top of right bust.

Edging:

Starting at top right of back neckline where the right strap attaches and with smaller hook, rejoin yarn and sl st along top edge of back, the sc up and over strap edge, then sl st along front neckline, then sc up and over opposite strap edge to beginning of edging. Sl st to 1st st to join. Fasten off

Starting to the left of where left strap attaches to back, sl st along left underarm, then sc up and over strap edge to beginning of edging. Sl st to 1st st to join. Fasten off.

Starting to the left of where right strap attaches to front, sl st along right underarm, then sc up and over strap edge to beginning of edging. Sl st to 1st st to join. Fasten off.

Secure and weave in all ends.

Bonita Easy Halter Top

59

MATERIALS

– cotton Dk weight yarn. Use around 500-600 yard.
– 3.0 mm crochet hook
– Sewing yarn needle
-stitch marker

Gauge:

4 double crochet stitch x 4 row = 1 inch

Finished Size Approximately:

S-XL easy to adjust
This crochet halter top is made in size small to medium.
The other sizes are easy to adjust by just add more chain to
make it wider . see pattern detail below for bigger size.
This top is made from top down.
We will make this summer top from top to bottom.
Front panel.

PATTERN

Start by Pick up crochet hook size 3.0 mm and Start of by making a slip knot
Then make 20 chains (All size) (foundation chain in even number)

Row 1: make 1dc in the next chain from hook and across until the end of the
row, ch2 turn.

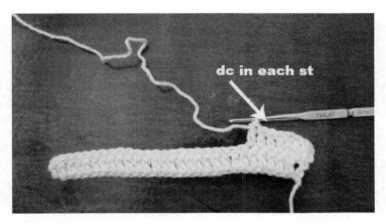

Row 2. now you will work 2dc in first stitch then 1dc in each stitch across until
end of the row on the last st make 2dc. ch2 turn.

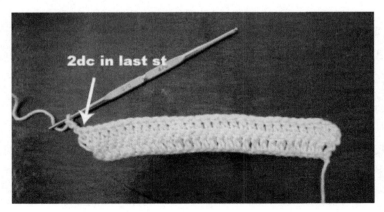

Row 3. now you will work 2dc in first stitch then 1dc in each stitch across until end of the row on the last st make 2dc. ch2 turn.

Row 4-13. repeat row3.

On this row14. we will start to make a body of the top.

Row 14. now you will work 2dc in first stitch then 1dc in each stitch across until end of the row on the last st make 2dc. then ch10 on each side(size small to medium) turn.

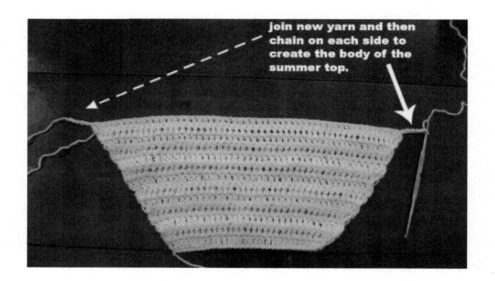

join new yarn and then chain on each side to create the body of the summer top.

then ch10 (size small to medium) cut the yarn off and join new yarn at the other side then add the same number of chain on the other side or you can add more chain to increase your size that will fit you bust.

ch18 (size large) turn.

ch 24 (size XL) turn.

Row 15: make 1dc in the next chain from hook and in each st across until the end of the row, ch2 turn.

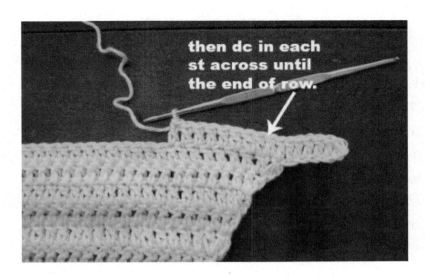

Row 16: make 1dc in the next stitch from hook and across until the end of the row, ch2 turn.

Row 17 and beyond ,....Repeat row 16 until you get 5 inch long. or your desired length and we will start to making lace bottom.

Row 1 of lace. ch2,*dc in next st , ch1 ,skip1, dc in next* repeat * to * across until the end of he row.

Row 2 of lace. ch2,*dc in each st ,* repeat * to * across until the end of the row.

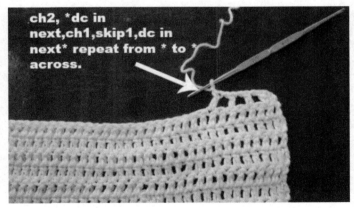

Back panel.

Start by chain the number that match with your front panel.

Row 1. dc in each chain across. ch2 turn.

Row 2. 1dc in each st across, ch2 turn.

Row 3 and beyond ,....Repeat row 2 until you get 5 inch long. or your desired length and we will start to making lace bottom.

Row 1 of lace. ch2,*dc in next st , ch1 ,skip1, dc in next* repeat * to * across until the end of he row.

Row 2 of lace. ch2,*dc in each st ,* repeat * to * across until the end of the row.

Assembly.

Lay back panel on top of front panel.
then sew on the each side.
Time to make the edge pretty.
Making the edge.

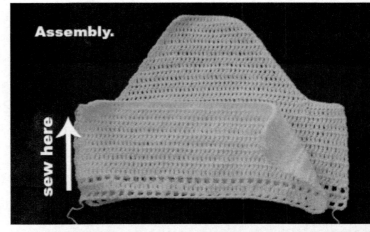

Make sc around the edge 2 round.
then make ch2, *1dc, ch1, skip1,
then 1dc in next st.* repeat this *
to * around the edge.

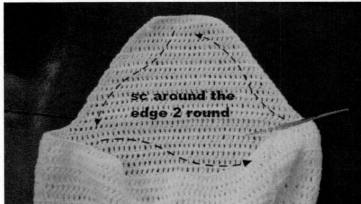

Then make dc in each st around.

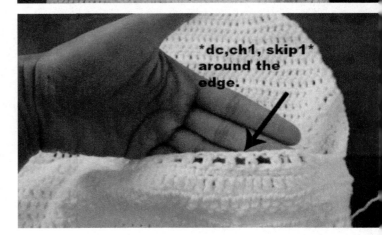

65

Making Strap.

Join new yarn at this side then chain 70 to 80 depend on how it fit u.
Then sc in each chain across. ch2 turn
Then * 1dc,ch1, skip1 and dc in next st* repeat this * to * across.
And repeat this process on the other side.

join new yarn at the point then chain 100-12 depend on your fit.

then use yarn needle to attach the strap to the back panel.

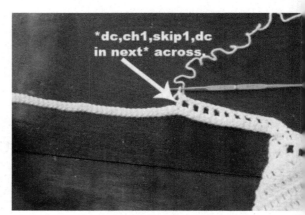

dc,ch1,skip1,dc in next across.

All done!

Country Festival Top

MATERIALS

Needle Size: 4mm hook, or size needed to obtain gauge
Yarn: Medium weight 4 yarn. Sample crocheted in Lily Sugar'n Cream. Approx 171 (215, 230, 250, 350) yards.

Gauge:

14.7 st/ 9 rows in hdc = 4"

Approximate Cup Sizes:

S: 34A, 32B, 34B, 30C, M: 36A, 38A, 36B, 32C, 34C, 30D, 32D, 30DD, L: 40A, 38B, 40B, 36C, 34D, 32DD, 34DD, 30DDD, 32DDD, XL: 38C, 40C, 36D, 38D, 40D, 36DD, 34DDD, 2XL: 38DD, 40DD, 36DDD, 38DDD, 40DDD
Model Sizing: model has 35" bust, wears a 34B cup, and is wearing the S size.

PATTERN

BRA CUPS

Approx sizes (width x height):
Before Border
S: 6" x 6.5"
M: 6.5" x 7.25"
L: 7.25" x 7.75"
XL: 8" x 8.5"
2XL: 8.75" x 9"
After Cup Decoration:
S: 7" x 7"
M: 7.5" x 7.75"
L: 8.25" x 8.25"
XL: 9" x 9"
2XL: 9.75" x 9.5"
Cup 1:
Ch13 (15, 13, 15, 13)

Row 1: hdc in 3rd ch from hook (counts as 1 dc), 9 (11, 9, 11, 9) hdc down ch, 5hdcshell in last ch, turn piece and 10 (12, 10, 12, 10) hdc working down the back side of ch. Turn. (Each row increases by 4st. 25, 29, 25, 29, 25 st)

Row 2: ch2 (does not count as st), hdc in each hdc below until center st of 5hdcshell, 5hdcshell into center st, hdc in each hdc to end. (Make sure you don't add a st here). Turn.

Row 3 -7(8, 9, 10, 11): cont. in same manner as Row 2 until you have the correct sized cup. (49, 57, 57, 65, 65 st)

FO

Cup 2:

Rep Row 1 - 7(8, 9, 10, 11)

FO

If you feel like you need more coverage, go ahead and work one or more rows into the cups until you like the coverage

BOTTOM PANEL AND BACK TIES:

Ch 70(70, 80, 80, 100).
Attach ch to bottom of bra cup with a sc (counts as 1 sc), then sc evenly along the bottom of the cup in multiples of 4, ch1, attach to 2nd cup with sc (counts as 1 sc) and then sc evenly along bottom of 2nd cup in multiples of 4. (multiples of 4 +3)
Ch70(70, 80, 80, 100)
FO

attach ch here

work toward cups

Row 1: starting at the 21(21, 25, 25, 29) ch from the right hand cup, working towards the cup, attach yarn and ch3 (does not count as a st). Dc in same ch, dc in each ch across towards cup, dc in each sc across 1st cup, 1 dc in ch between cups, dc in each sc across next cup, and dc in the ch until 21(21, 25, 25, 29) ch after 2nd cup. (You should end up with a multiple of 4 sts +1). Turn.
For M and L: make one more row of dc. (2 total)
For XL and 2XL: make two more rows of dc (3 total)
If you feel you might need more support for larger breasts, repeat Row 1 as many times as needed
Row 2(3, 3, 4, 4): ch3 (count as a st), 3dc into same st, [sk3, 4dcshell in next st] rep [ ] across placing last 4dcshell in last dc of previous row. Turn.
Row 3(4, 4, 5, 5): ch6, *sk 3, sc in next st, ch5* (be careful not to miss the 1st st) rep * * across, sk3, place last sc in ch3 of previous row. Turn.
Row 4(5, 5, 6, 6): *Ch 5, sc in ch 5 space* rep * * across row, sc in 1st ch of ch6 of previous row. Turn.

Row 5(6, 6, 7, 7): *Ch 5, sc in ch 5 space* across. Turn.
Row 6(7, 7, 8, 8): rep Row 4
Row 7(8, 8, 9, 9): ch3, 4dc in each ch5 across to last ch5, dc in1st ch of the last ch5 of previous row.
Do Not Fasten Off. Turn 90 degrees.

CUP DECORATION AND FINISHING:

Ch1
Row 1: sc evenly up side to long ch, place 3 sc in the back side of the 1st dc on ch, turn 90 degrees, sc in back of dc towards cups, at cups, [ch2, sk1, sc in next st] around cup, until last 4 st on 1st cup, ch1, sc in the 4th st of opposite cup, rep [ ] around 2nd cup, sc in back of dc towards end, place 3 sc in back side of last dc, turn 90 degrees and sc evenly down final side.
FO
If the connector ch1 st does not land on the 4th to last st on the right side bra cup, you missed the first st on the cup

Row 2: Reattach yarn at bottom of right side cup in the first ch2 from previous row w/ a sl st, [sc, ch3, sc] all in ch2 space, cont. [ ] around both cups placing one [ ] in the ch1 between cups as well.
FO
For larger breasts, if you feel you need a little more structure for your top or want to pull the top closed at the front, you can sc the picots together that are 6th from the center on each cup.

Sea Breeze Tank Top

*The sizing guide follows size XS(S, M, L, XL, 2XL, 3XL). E.g. "Ch 32(36, 40, 44, 48, 52, 56) means Ch 32 for XS, Ch 36 for Small, Ch 40 for Medium, Ch 44 for Large, Ch 48 for XL, Ch 52 for 2XL and Ch 56 for 3XL
*When there is only one number, e.g. Ch 7, this number applies to all sizes
*Total number of stitches is listed between < >
*"DC 10" means DC into the next 10 stitches
*"2DC" means place 2 DC into the same stitch
*Ch 2 and Ch 1 does NOT count as a stitch
*This pattern uses US crochet terms
*Sample is a size small shown on a 5'3" model with a 32" bust.
*This top is designed for the V to fall directly in middle of the bust area. To have more coverage/the V to be higher, I recommend working to Rows 2 – 4 instead of Rows 2 - 6 when creating the straps.

MATERIALS:

Yarn – Debbie Bliss Cotton Denim DK – DK (8 ply), 200m/100g, 100% Cotton in Pale Blue
Skeins – 2(2, 3, 4, 4, 5, 5)
4.5mm (US 7) Crochet Hook
Darning Needle
Scissors

GAUGE:

10cm/4" square = 13 stitches wide x 9 rows tall in double crochet

PATTERN

LEFT TRIANGLE

*Once you've finished your left triangle, I highly recommend trying it on/holding it up to your body as bust size can vary greatly within the same size – you may need to size up or size down.

FOUNDATION CHAIN: Ch 7.

ROW 1: DC into the 3rd chain from the hook, DC 4. <5>

ROWS 2-6: Ch 2, turn, DC 5. <5>

ROW 7: Ch 2, turn, 2DC, DC 4. <6>

ROW 8: Ch 2, turn, DC 5, 2DC. <7>

ROW 9: Ch 2, turn, 2DC, DC 5, 2DC. <9>

ROW 10: Ch 2, turn, DC 8, 2DC. <10>

ROW 11: Ch 2, turn, 2DC, DC 9. <11>

ROW 12: Ch 2, turn, DC 10, 2DC. <12>

ROW 13: Ch 2, turn, 2DC, 2DC, DC 10. <14>

ROW 14: Ch 2, turn, 2DC, DC 11, 2DC, 2DC. <17>

ROW 15: Ch 2, turn, 2DC, DC 15, 2DC. <19>

ROW 16: Ch 2, turn, 2DC, DC 17, 2DC. <21>

*Size XS – Fasten off. Proceed to Right Triangle instructions.

Sizes (S, M, L, XL, 2XL, 3XL)

ROW 17: Ch 2, turn, 2DC, 2DC, DC 18, 2DC. <24>

ROW 18: Ch 2, turn, 2DC, DC 22, 2DC. <26>

*Size S – Fasten off. Proceed to Right Triangle instructions.

Sizes (M, L, XL, 2XL, 3XL)

ROW 19: Ch 2, turn, 2DC, 2DC, DC until last st, 2DC into last stitch. <29>

ROW 20: Ch 2, turn, 2DC, DC until last 2 sts, 2DC, 2DC. <32>

*Size M – Fasten off. Proceed to Right Triangle instructions.
Sizes (L, XL, 2XL, 3XL) repeat ROWS 19-20 until ROW (22, 24, 26, 28).
<38, 44, 50, 56>
Fasten off. Proceed to Right Triangle instructions.

RIGHT TRIANGLE

FOUNDATION CHAIN: Ch 7.
ROW 1: DC into the 3rd chain from the hook, DC 4. <5>
ROWS 2-6: Ch 2, turn, DC 5. <5>
ROW 7: Ch 2, turn, DC 4, 2DC. <6>
ROW 8: Ch 2, turn, 2DC, DC 5. <7>
ROW 9: Ch 2, turn, 2DC, DC 5, 2DC. <9>
ROW 10: Ch 2, turn, 2DC, DC 8. <10>
ROW 11: Ch 2, turn, DC 9, 2DC. <11>
ROW 12: Ch 2, turn, 2DC, DC 10. <12>
ROW 13: Ch 2, turn, DC 10, 2DC, 2DC. <14>
ROW 14: Ch 2, turn, 2DC, 2DC, DC 11, 2DC. <17>
ROW 15: Ch 2, turn, 2DC, DC 15, 2DC. <19>
ROW 16: Ch 2, turn, 2DC, DC 17, 2DC. <21>
*Size XS – do not fasten off! Proceed directly to Joining Row instructions.
Sizes (S, M, L, XL, 2XL, 3XL)
ROW 17: Ch 2, turn, 2DC, DC 18, 2DC, 2DC. <24>
ROW 18: Ch 2, turn, 2DC, DC 22, 2DC. <26>
*Size S – do not fasten off! Proceed directly to Joining Row instructions.
Sizes (M, L, XL, 2XL, 3XL)
ROW 19: Ch 2, turn, 2DC, DC until last 2 sts, 2DC, 2DC. <29>

ROW 20: Ch 2, turn, 2DC, 2DC, DC until last st, 2DC into the last st. <32>
*Size M – do not fasten off! Proceed directly to Joining Row instructions.
Sizes (L, XL, 2XL, 3XL) repeat ROWS 19-20 until ROW (22, 24, 26, 28).
<38, 44, 50, 56>
Do not fasten off! Proceed directly to Joining Row instructions.

JOINING ROW

JOINING ROW: Ch 2, turn, 2DC, 2DC, DC 18(23, 29, 35, 41, 47, 53, 59), 2DC into last st of Right Triangle.
<24, 29, 35, 41, 47, 53, 59>
Place the Left Triangle (with the right side facing up) to the left of the Right Triangle.
2DC into the first st of the Left Triangle, DC 18(23, 29, 35, 41, 47, 53, 59), 2DC, 2DC.
<48, 58, 70, 82, 94, 106, 118>

BODY

BODY ROW 1: Ch 2, turn, 2DC, 2DC, DC in each st until the last 2 sts, 2DC, 2DC.
<52, 62, 74, 86, 98, 110, 122>
BODY ROW 2: Ch 2, turn, DC in each st until the end of the row.
<52, 62, 74, 86, 98, 110, 122>
Repeat BODY ROW 2 until ROW 13.
*You can add or remove rows to reach yor desired length – please keep in mind that the ribbing adds 2cm/0.75".

RIBBING

ROW 1: Ch 1, turn, SC in each st until the end of the row.
<52, 62, 74, 86, 98, 110, 122>
ROW 2: Ch 2, turn, *FpDC into the next 2 sts, BpDC into the next 2 sts; rep from * until last 2 sts, FpDC, DC.
<52, 62, 74, 86, 98, 110, 122>
ROW 3: Ch 2, turn, DC, BpDC, *FpDC 2, BpDC 2; rep from * until end, DC into the 2nd chain (at the beginning of ROW 2).
<53, 63, 75, 87, 99, 111, 123>
*The extra DC at the end helps the edges of the top stay straight and neat.
Repeat all steps for the 2nd side of the top.

ASSEMBLY

Lay the 2 pieces of the top directly on top of each other. Sew the straps and the sides off the top together.

FINISHING

At the bottom of an armhole, insert hook, secure yarn and pull up a loop.

Ch 1, SC evenly along the edge of the armhole, making sure that your stitches are not too tight.

Sl st into first SC to join. Fasten off.

Repeat for the 2nd armhole.

Insert hook along the V-neck, secure yarn and pull up a loop.

Ch 1, SC evenly along the edge of the V-neck, making sure that your stitches are not too tight.

Sl st into first SC to join. Fasten off.

Weave in all of your ends. You've finished your Sea Breeze Tank Top!

Eden Crop Top

MEASUREMENTS

This pattern follows sizes S(M, L, XL)
GAUGE: 15 sc by 21 rows using 5mm hook

MATERIALS

- Yarn – Paintbox Cotton Dk – light/weight 3/DK/8 ply ~ 50g/ 1.8oz/125m/137yds
- Approximately 4(4, 5, 5) balls
- Other yarn suggestions Drops Cotton Light
- 3.5mm crochet hook
- 5mm crochet hook
- Stitch marker
- Scissors
- Yarn needle

PATTERN

Using 3.5mm hook
Ch 16
Row 1: sc in 2nd ch from hook, sc in each ch to end. Turn.
Row 2: ch 1, sc in BLO in each st across. Turn.
Repeat row 2 until you reach row 102(110, 118, 126).
Slst the two ends together to form a circle. We will now be working in rounds.

Change to 5mm crochet hook

Round 1: ch 1, make 102(110, 118, 126) sc evenly around the top edge of ribbing. TURN.
Round 2: ch 1, sc in each st around. TURN.
Repeat round 2 until you have completed round 16(18, 20, 22). TURN
Mark the 51st(55th, 59th, 63rd) st.
Continuing on from where you are now:
Next row: ch 1, sc2tog, sc in each st across until you reach the second st from st marker, sc2tog. Turn.
Next row: ch 1, sc2tog, sc in each st across until 2 sts remain, sc2tog. Turn.
You should now have 47(51, 55, 59) sts.
Now mark the 23rd(25th, 27th, 29th) st.
Next row: ch 1 sc across to st marker. Turn.
Next row: ch 1, sc2tog, sc in each st until 2 sts remain, sc2tog. Turn.
Next row: ch 1, sc in each st across. Turn.
Next row: ch 1, sc2tog, sc in each st across until 2 sts remain, sc2tog. Turn.
Rep last 2 rows until 3 sts remain. Turn.

Next row: ch 1 sc in each of the 3 sts. Turn.

Next row: ch 1, sc3tog. Turn.

Next row: ch 1, sc in that last st.

Fasten off.

For the 2nd "triangle":

Skip the st directly beside the last "triangle and attach yarn to the next st.

Next row: ch 1, sc in each of the next 23(25, 27, 29) sts.

Next row: ch 1, sc2tog, sc in each st across until 2 sts remain, sc2tog. Turn.

Next row: ch 1, sc in each st across. Turn.

Next row: ch 1, sc2tog, sc in each st across until 2 sts remain, sc2tog. Turn.

Rep last 2 rows until 3 sts remain. Turn.

Next row: ch 1, sc in each of next 2 sts. Turn.

Next row: ch 1, sc3tog. Turn.

Next row: ch 1, sc in last remaining st.

Fasten off.

Now turn your work and begin working on the two back "triangles".

You should have 51(55, 59, 63) unworked here.

Attach your yarn to the stitch next to triangle that you just finished.

Next row: ch 1, sc2tog, sc in each st across until 2 sts remain, sc2tog. Turn.

Next row: ch 1, sc2tog, sc in each st across until 2 sts remain, sc2tog. Turn.

Mark the 23rd(25th, 27th, 29th) st.

Next row: ch 1, sc in each st across until you reach marker. Turn.

Next row: ch 1, sc2tog, sc in each st across until 2 sts remain, sc2tog. Turn.

Next row: ch 1, sc in each st across. Turn.

Next row: ch 1, sc2tog, sc in each st across until 2 sts remain, sc2tog. Turn.

Rep last 2 rows until 3 sts remain. Turn.

Next row: ch 1, sc in each of 3 sts. Turn.
Next row: ch 1, sc3tog. Turn.
Next row: ch 1, sc in last remaining st.
Fasten off.
Now we make the 2nd back "triangle"
Skip the st directly beside the triangle just worked and attach yarn to the next st.
Next row: ch 1, sc in each of remaining 23(25, 27, 29) sts. Turn.
Next row: ch 1, sc2tog, sc in each st across until 2 sts remain, sc2tog. Turn.
Next row: ch 1, sc in each st across. Turn.
Next row: ch 1, sc2tog, sc in each st across until 2 sts remain, sc2tog. Turn.
Rep last 2 rows until 3 sts remain. Turn.
Next row: ch 1, sc in each of the 3 sts. Turn.
Next row: ch 1, sc3tog. Turn.
Next row: ch 1, sc in last remaining st. DO NOT FASTEN OFF
Next row: ch 1 and sc all the way around the 4 triangles. Slst to first sc you made.

Change to 3.5mm crochet hook
**Ch 5, sc in 2nd ch from hook, sc in next 3 chains, slst in next 2 sc on the side of "triangle", * turn, skip 2 slsts, sc in BLO in each of next 4 sts, turn, ch 1, sc in BLO in next 4 sts, slst in next 2 sc on side of "triangle", rep from * all the way around arrmhole until you reach the peak of the triangle directly behind. Fasten off.
Attach yarn to the peak of the other front "triangle and rep from **.
Next attach yarn to the unworked middle st between the two front "triangles"

****Ch 5, sc in 2nd ch from hook, sc in next 3 chains, slst in next 2 sc on side of "triangle,* turn, skip 2 slsts, sc in BLO in next 4 sts, turn, ch 1 sc in BLO in next 4 sts, slst in next 2 sc on side of triangle, rep from * all the way up along the inner edge of the triangle. The top of the triangle should be worked like shown in photo below.

Next row: ch 1, turn. Sc in BLO of next 2 slsts, sc in BLO in next 4 sc. Turn (6 sc).

Next row: ch 1, sc in BLO in each of next 6 sc. Turn.

Rep last row until you have a further 24 rows completed. Fasten off leaving a long tail.****

Now attach your yarn to the next available middle st between the two front triangles and rep from **** to ****.

Now it's time to work the ribbing towards the back of the top. This is done in the same way as the front so just follow those steps again but when you finish the straps on this side there is no need to leave a long tail when fastening off.

Now with your tail and yarn needle make a few sts to secure the inner "v" ribbing like shown below on both the front and back of the top.

Now turn your top wrong side out and with your yarn needle and long tail, stitch the front (shoulder)strap to the back strap creating one continuous strap. Rep on the other side.

You are now finished making your Eden Crop Top.

Fold this side

Over this side

Printed in Great Britain
by Amazon